WORLDVIEW GUIDE

MEDITATIONS *of Marcus Aurelius*

Dr. Brian Phillips

canonpress
Moscow, Idaho

Published by Canon Press
P.O. Box 8729, Moscow, Idaho 83843
800.488.2034 | www.canonpress.com

Dr. Brian Phillips, *Worldview Guide for the Meditations of Marcus Aurelius*
Copyright ©2019 by Brian Phillips.
Cited page numbers come from the Canon Classics edition of the book (2017),
www.canonpress.com/books/canon-classics.

Cover design by James Engerbretson
Cover illustration by Forrest Dickison
Interior design by Valerie Anne Bost and James Engerbretson

Printed in the United States of America.

Library of Congress Cataloging-in-Publication Data
Phillips, Brian (Educator and Clergy), author.
Meditations of Marcus Aurelius worldview guide / Brian Phillips.
Moscow, Idaho : Canon Press, [2019].
LCCN 2019011336 | ISBN 9781944503888 (pbk. : alk. paper)
LCSH: Marcus Aurelius, Emperor of Rome, 121-180. Meditations.
Classification: LCC B583 .P45 2019 | DDC 188--dc23
LC record available at https://lccn.loc.gov/2019011336

A free end-of-book test and answer key are available for download at
www.canonpress.com/ClassicsQuizzes

19 20 21 22 23 24   9 8 7 6 5 4 3 2 1

CONTENTS

INTRODUCTION

What if you could spy into the mind of a great world leader? Uncover what made them tick? See what motivated them? Learn to understand why they made the decisions they made? Emperor Marcus Aurelius' *Meditations* allow you to do just that, and the wisdom found in them is astounding.

The *Meditations* were not written under contract from a publisher. Aurelius had no literary agent and went on no book tours. From what we can tell, there was no intention that these sayings would ever be read by another soul. Rather, they were the emperor's personal notes on how to think, how to lead, and how to live.

THE WORLD AROUND

Emperor Marcus Aurelius wrote his *Meditations* during his nineteen-year reign from A.D. 161–180, a complex time for the Roman Empire. Soon after taking power, Marcus and his army were at war with the Parthians, who attempted to invade Roman territory, threatening much of Syria and Armenia.

When the armies returned, after successful campaigns, they inadvertently brought serious sickness with them, resulting in a plague that enveloped much of Rome in 166 and continued for about three years.

With the army stretched thin due to the plague, Rome faced yet another uprising, this time by the Quadi and other tribes along the Danube. It was during these military campaigns that Marcus wrote much of his *Meditations*.

The second century was turbulent for the Church as well, with Christianity not being recognized as a legal religion. Persecution was typically local and sporadic, but it was during this century that Polycarp, the 86-year-old bishop of Smyrna, was martyred for his faith in Christ. This gave rise to some of the great early Christian apologists like Justin Martyr and Irenaeus. The Church also struggled against internal turmoil in the form of heresies like Gnosticism, Montanism, and Marcionism.

Gnostics claimed the all things existed in a kind of dualism—part good (the spiritual world) and part evil (the material world)—and they possessed a secret spiritual knowledge of how man and God could be reconciled. Montanists claimed special revelations, visions, and prophecies; almost a second-century charismatic movement. Marcion taught that Christianity was entirely separate from Judaism, and rejected the Old Testament. Responding to these heresies, along with persecution from outside the Church, created difficulties for second-century Christians, but the Church grew stronger and more organized nonetheless.

In much lighter news, the second century also brought about the cultivation of the potato by farmers in the Peruvian Andes (around A.D. 200)!

ABOUT THE AUTHOR

Over the course of his life, Marcus had three different names. At birth, he was named Marcus Annius Verus. But, upon his adoption as heir by Emperor Antoninus Pius, he was renamed Marcus Aelius Aurelius Verus. Finally, after becoming Emperor of Rome, the full title of Imperator Caesar Marcus Aurelius Antoninus Augustus was bestowed.

Marcus's adoption by Pius arose as a matter of legal and political expediency, not of affection. "For the Roman emperors, it was a useful way to combine the great advantage of a father-to-son succession (it was always perfectly clear who the next emperor was supposed to be) with the great republican notion that only the deserving should have power. Adoption allowed each emperor to pass his throne not to the son he had, but to the son he had hoped for."[1]

---

1. Susan Wise Bauer, *The History of the Ancient World* (New York: W.W. Norton, 2007), 751-752.

At the age of forty, Marcus reluctantly took power after Pius' death. In his excellent biography of Marcus, Anthony Birley writes that he had to be "compelled by the senate to assume the direction of the state after the death of Pius."[2] Marcus was far more interested in philosophy than politics and, though he had performed his previously required political duties, he did not relish them.

However, it was his devotion to Stoic philosophy, with its emphasis on duty and right conduct, that would lead Marcus to choose duty over personal preference. He wrote, "Let it make no difference to thee whether thou art cold or warm, if thou art doing thy duty; and whether thou art drowsy or satisfied with sleep; and whether ill-spoken of or praised; and whether dying or doing something else. For it is one of the acts of life, this act by which we die: it is sufficient then in this act also to do well what we have in hand" (*Meditations* VI.4).[3] Further, "Adapt thyself to the things with which thy lot has been cast: and the men among whom thou hast received thy portion, love them, but do it truly" (VI.39).

And so, Marcus performed his duty as emperor, along with his brother Lucius Verus whom Marcus appointed as co-emperor. He was beloved by the people of Rome,

---

2. Anthony Birley, *Marcus Aurelius: A Biography* (London: Routledge, 2002), 116.

3. All quotations are from the Canon Classics edition of *Meditations* (Moscow, ID: Canon Press, 2017), which was translated by George Long in 1862.

protected the empire during several border wars, and when those wars posed a financial threat to the empire, he bolstered the treasury by selling the goods of his own palace rather than raising taxes. Marcus would thus be called the last of the Good Emperors.

WHAT OTHER
NOTABLES SAID

Philip Schaff, author of the eight-volume *History of the Christian Church*, labeled "Marcus Aurelius, the last and best representative of Stoicism...."[4]

Susan Wise Bauer calls the *Meditations* "one of the classics of Stoicism. They are the musings of a man trapped by his own duty, carrying the weight of an empire that he was happiest when farthest from."[5]

In his essay "Marcus Aurelius," Matthew Arnold wrote, "[W]hen one turns over the pages of his *Meditations*,—entries jotted down from day to day, amid the business of the city or the fatigues of the camp, for his own guidance and support, meant for no eye but his own, without the slightest attempt at style, with no care, even, for correct

---

4. Philip Schaff, *History of the Christian Church*, vol. 2, *Ante-Nicene Christianity* (New York: Charles Scribner's Sons, 1910), 326.

5. Bauer, *The History of the Ancient World*, 754.

writing, not to be surpassed for naturalness and sinceri-ty,—all disposition to carp and cavil dies away, and one is overpowered by the charm of a character of such purity, delicacy, and virtue. He fails neither in small things nor in great; he keeps watch over himself both that the great springs of action may be right in him, and that the minute details of action may be right also."

C. Scott Hicks and David V. Hicks, in the Introduction of their book *The Emperor's Handbook*, wrote, "It is fine for scholars to study Marcus, but it is *natural* for the captains of industry and armies to carry him in their briefcases, for this was a man of action, not merely of words, and the few words he wrote to himself were meant to incite action, not dissertations."[6]

---

6. *The Emperor's Handbook: A New Translation of The Meditations*, (New York: Scribner, 2002), 4.

SETTING, STRUCTURE, AND THEMES

Setting

As previously mentioned, Marcus showed little interest in political power. The anonymous author of *Lives of the Later Caesars* (circa 4th century) wrote that Marcus, "was serious-minded from his earliest childhood.... He took a passionate interest in philosophy even when still a boy: when he had entered his twelfth year he dressed himself in the philosopher's standard clothing and then began to practice endurance of hardship as philosopher's do. He began to do his studies in a Greek cloak and used to sleep on the ground."[7]

Even when he was later "compelled" to govern as emperor, he "nominated his brother as joint emperor with himself. He gave him the name of Lucius Aurelius Verus

---

7. *Lives of the Later Caesars*, trans. Anthony Birley (New York: Penguin Books, 1976), 109-110.

Commodus and the titles of Caesar and Augustus, and from that moment they began to govern the republic jointly."[8] Such a move was unprecedented in Roman government, powerfully demonstrating that Marcus' reluctance to rule was no mere put-on.

So devout was Marcus' love of philosophy that he penned much of his *Meditations* even while leading his troops in the Marcomannic Wars (circa A.D. 166–180). The last line of Book I says he penned those words "Among the Quadi," a tribe which Marcus battled during his reign. Book II ends with a note that its contents were penned "in Carnuntum," where Marcus and his men fought in the second Marcomannic War around A.D. 178. True to the Stoic ideal, Marcus gave himself to the pursuit of virtue in this life, even when surrounded by battle.

Not only was Marcus the last of the Good Emperors, he was a model of the philosopher-king. His *Meditations* are the result of that lifelong pursuit of wisdom and virtue, which the Stoics saw as man's highest calling.

Structure

The *Meditations* follow very little organization, outside of Book I. Some scholars believe Book I might have been written last, to scrve as a kind of introduction to the rest of the work.[9] The remainder is quite disjointed, covering

---

8. Ibid., 115.

9. See C.R. Haines's introductory essays for the Loeb Classical Library edition of *Meditations* (Cambridge, MA: Harvard University Press,

a wide variety of topics, sometimes in lengthy paragraphs, and sometimes in single sentences.

The lack of organization or outline arises from the fact that the *Meditations* were written for Marcus himself. They were a kind of journal or diary, focusing on what it means to live a life of virtue. It seems likely that Marcus simply penned his thoughts as he had them, whether they arose from the circumstances of life or from the influence of his teachers and their writings.

Given that the *Meditations* was written primarily for Marcus' personal reflection, he mentions few other people, with the exception of Book I, which opens with "thank you" list to those who had great impact on his life—from family members to teachers.

Themes

Reading a classic work, like the *Meditations* of Marcus Aurelius, is not a "static" activity. Classic literature involves us in a great conversation in which the reader must wrestle with the themes, questions, and arguments of the book. As you encounter the following themes (and any others you notice) in the book, work to articulate what Marcus says about them, and be able to interact with and respond to his ideas:

- Man and God (or gods)
- Fate and free will
- Duty and personal responsibility

1916), xiiff.

- Self-control
- Gratitude & contentment
- Difficult people & circumstances
- Time and priorities
- Personal discipline
- Manhood
- Sorrow and happiness

UNDERSTANDING WISDOM LITERATURE

Before we turn to the book itself, the genre of the *Meditations* requires a few notes. Wisdom literature is a genre of literature marked by the sayings of wise teachers, typically focused on what it means to live well and what it means to know God (or the gods, depending on the writer). Such writings were relatively common in the Ancient Near East and include the Old Testament books of Job, Psalms, Proverbs, Ecclesiastes, and the Song of Solomon, as well as the apocryphal books of Sirach and the Book of Wisdom.

However, the genre is not confined to the Ancient Near East. If one applies the term "wisdom literature" more broadly, the genre could include writings like Confucius' *Analects*, Sun Tzu's *The Art of War*, St. Augustine's *Confessions*, Benjamin Franklin's *Poor Richard's Almanack*, and of course, Marcus Aurelius' *Meditations*.

But, even if one uses very wide parameters for wisdom literature, Marcus' *Meditations* are unique to the Greco-Roman world. In *Christianity and Classical Culture*, Charles Norris Cochrane wrote: "It is indeed a suggestive truth that, in more than a thousand years of literary history, the Greco-Roman world had failed to produce anything which might justly be called a personal record; in this sense, Augustine (with his *Confessions*) was perhaps anticipated only by the emperor Marcus Aurelius."[10]

Because wisdom literature is comprised largely of maxims and proverbs, one cannot expect it to read as a novel would, or any other genre. In wisdom writings, one section may have little connection to the ones before or after it, meaning the reader must simply follow where the writer takes him. Themes or common ideas may be found in wisdom literature, but they must be searched for diligently, as they may be visible only after reading the entire work. For example, in Proverbs, King Solomon wrote frequently about the power of words, but he rarely did so in sequential verses.

Finally, another helpful practice with wisdom literature is comparing two passages in the same work, or comparing passages from two different works of wisdom literature. This is enlightening and helps the reader understand even subtle similarities and differences.

---

10. Charles Norris Cochrane, *Christianity and Classical Culture: a study of thought and action from Augustus to Augustine* (Oxford: OUP, 1957), 427.

WORLDVIEW ANALYSIS

Take pleasure in one thing and rest in it, in passing
from one social act (that is, an act of kindness) to
another social act, thinking of God. (VI.7)

How has thou behaved hitherto to the gods, thy
parents, brethren, children, teachers, to those who
looked after thy infancy, to thy friends, kinsfolk, to
thy slaves? Consider if thou has hitherto behaved
to all in such a way that this might be said of thee,
"Never has wronged a man in deed or word." (V.31)

Such lines from the *Meditations* stand out as powerful
examples of just how "Christian" Marcus Aurelius could
sound at times. Church historian Philip Schaff wrote that
Marcus was "nearly approaching a disciple of Jesus. We
must admire his purity, truthfulness, philanthropy, con-
scientious devotion to duty, his serenity of mind in the
midst of temptations of power and severe domestic trials,

and his resignation to the will of providence. He was fully appreciated in his time, and universally beloved by his subjects. We may well call him among the heathen the greatest and best man of his age."[11]

Marcus was not a Christian, however, and his philosophy left him little room to understand their doctrine and way of life, leaving Christian readers with quite a puzzle when approaching his life and writings.

Stoicism

What comes to mind when you hear the word "stoic"? For most people, "stoic" simply means serious, unemotional, or perhaps unconcerned with events around them. Unfortunately, these ideas do not fully capture what it meant to be a Stoic—that is, a follower of Stoic philosophy, as Marcus Aurelius was. Again, Schaff writes that the emperor was "mild, amiable, gentle; in these respects the very reverse of a hard and severe Stoic…"[12]

So, what was Stoicism? What did they believe? The beliefs of Stoics varied a bit, but there are certain elements they seem to have held in common.

First, Stoics believed, as Seneca the Younger, an influential Stoic writer, is known for saying, "Virtue is its own reward." It is enough to attain goodness in this life, whether or not we have the promise of reward in the afterlife.

---

11. Philip Schaff, *History of the Christian Church*, 2:327.
12. Ibid., 2:327.

Second, virtue required submission to God or the gods. This meant not allowing our desires to master us, but rather submitting to whatever the gods required of us, regardless of our own wishes.

Connected with the second, Stoics held a strong view of what would be called providence by some, fatalism by others. Epictetus, another influential Stoic, wrote, "I have submitted my freedom of choice unto God. He wills that I shall have fever; it is my will too." Note the combination of submission to the gods and resignation to the event, as if there is nothing else to be done.

Christianity & Stoicism

While there are certainly other details of Stoicism that could be considered, these few give us an indication of why Marcus could write passages that sounded so much like Christian thinking.

Christians put a high priority on personal godliness and virtue, but we do so with the sure hope of everlasting life and the promise that we are predestined to be made like Christ. In other words, for the Christian, it is not enough to attain virtue in this life, because our eternal souls are in need of redemption. "Goodness" in this life is simply not enough.

Further, Christians are taught to pray for God's will to be done "on earth, as it is in heaven." We are to place the will and plan of God above our own. But we do so within the context of a relationship with a personal God who knows and loves us, a God who hears our prayers. Stoicism held no such hope. Ultimately, Stoicism is a "religion of reason ... a kind of sky-writing which projects upon the cosmos a merely human rationality and translates it into an account of nature and of God."[13]

Marcus' *Meditations* is a tremendous work of wisdom literature—inspiring, challenging, and at times, closely resembling true Christian wisdom—but the differences between Stoicism and Christianity also become evident when comparing his work with that of St. Augustine or the Wisdom Books of the Bible. Again, Cochrane wrote, "while the work of Augustine was addressed to God, that of Aurelius was addressed to himself. In the *Meditations* the shadow of the great man lies for ever across the page.... The *Confessions*, on the other hand, are marked by a naïve simplicity; they betray not the most remote suggestion of pretension or priggishness."[14]

Unlike Augustine's intense spiritual honesty, Marcus "is concerned never to expose a weakness, remembering that it is his business to exemplify so far as possible the conventional type of excellence enshrined in the heroic ideal."[15] Marcus' search for the good life, to be the ideal man, is both honorable and somewhat tragic, because his pursuit is futile without Christ, the only ideal Man and the One in whom the just are made perfect (Hebrews 12:23).

---

13. *Christianity and Classical Culture*, 181.

14. Ibid., 427.

15. Ibid., 428.

Persecution of Christians

That Stoicism and Christianity were different was not lost on Marcus Aurelius. He only mentions Christians once in the *Meditations*, and not favorably.

> What a soul that is which is ready, if at any moment it must be separated from the body, and ready either to be extinguished or dispersed or continue to exist; but so that this readiness comes from a man's own judgment, *not from mere obstinacy, as with the Christians*, but considerately and with dignity and in a way to persuade another, without tragic show. (XI.3, emphasis mine)

He attributes the willingness of some Christians to face martyrdom as as a "tragic show" motivated by "mere obstinacy." It is unlikely that the emperor knew much of what Christians believed or what truly drove them to face death rather than recant their faith in Christ. Though several defenses of the faith were written to him, many believe it unlikely that he ever read them.[16]

Stoicism's emphasis on human reason, duty, and self-reliance would have made reports of the virgin birth, the Incarnation, miracles, and the Resurrection seem simply unbelievable. And so, the emperor who was among the best and wisest of men allowed Christians to be persecuted (sometimes brutally) during his reign. There was even a law against evangelism, "punishing every one with exile

---

16. Including Schaff, see *History of the Christian Church*, 2:53-54, 329-330.

who should endeavor to influence people's mind by fear of the Divinity, and this law was, no doubt, aimed at the Christians."[17]

Yet, even the seemingly clear-cut issue of persecution becomes complicated when we consider more of the historical context and the information Marcus may have been given by his advisors. For example, around the time of Marcus, the Church was involved in some debate about "spontaneous martyrs," who would willingly offer themselves to be killed. Some believed these were false martyrdoms and that martyrs were chosen by God, not by themselves.[18] It could be that the emperor's impression of Christians was colored by these spontaneous martyrs, causing him to see them as a strange sect with death wishes.

Additionally, the early days of Marcus' reign were marked with several disasters, like the rebellions and plague mentioned earlier, but also including the severe flooding of the Tiber River, which also led to food shortages. Soon, it was claimed that these tragedies were because the gods were angry with Rome for allowing Christianity to exist in the Empire. This type of explanation was not unusual, and Christians were targeted as scapegoats by Nero (for the Great Fire) and by Romans during the

---

17. Schaff, 2:54.

18. See Justo Gonzalez's *The Story of Christianity*, vol. 1, *The Early Church to the Dawn of the Reformation* (San Francisco: Harper & Row, 1984), 43-45.

days of St. Augustine (which prompted him to write *The City of God*, in defense of the Church).

It is at least possible that Marcus' approval for the persecution of Christians resulted from reports of spontaneous martyrs or his belief that the gods wanted Rome to rid itself of Christians.

What, then, should we think of him? Marcus was a wise man, but his wisdom was incomplete. He was a good man, by human standards. He pursued virtue, but could only attain a measure of it without Christ. In other words, he is a man we may learn from, even respect, but must also pity. He is an example of what God's common grace can do in greatly gifting and blessing a man, even when he remains an unbeliever. With great benefit, Christians can read the *Meditations* and learn, be challenged, and grow.

Christians have the particular blessing of being able to read classic literature with a more complete picture of the truth, goodness, and beauty demonstrated for us in the books, while at the same time seeing God's grace at work even in the stories and lives of pagans. We can see the flaws and perfections of Achilles, Odysseus, Aeneas, Beowulf, Dante, Hamlet, Marcus Aurelius, and more—learning from them both good and bad lessons that drive us to wisdom and virtue in Christ.

QUOTABLES

1. "Every moment think steadily as a Roman and a man to do what thou has in hand with perfect and simple dignity, and feeling of affection, and freedom, and justice, and to give thyself relief from all other thoughts."
   ~ Book II.5

2. "[T]hose who do not observe the movements of their own minds must of necessity be unhappy."
   ~ Book II.8

3. "For with what art thou discontented? With the badness of men? Recall to thy mind this conclusion, that rational animals exist for one another, and that to endure is a part of justice, and that men do wrong involuntarily; and consider how many already, after mutual enmity, suspicion, hatred, and fighting, have been stretched dead, reduced to ashes; and be quiet at last."
   ~ Book IV.3

4. "Never value anything as profitable to thyself which shall compel thee to break thy promise, to lose thy self-respect, to hate any man, to suspect, to curse, to act the hypocrite, to desire anything which needs wall and curtains…"

    ~ Book III.7

5. "It is in our power to have no opinion about a thing, and not to be disturbed in our soul; for things themselves have no natural power to form our judgments."

    ~ Book VI.52

6. "[E]very man is worth just so much as the things are worth about which he busies himself."

    ~ Book VII.3

7. "Take care not to feel towards the inhuman as they feel towards men."

    ~ Book VII.65

21 SIGNIFICANT
QUESTIONS AND ANSWERS

Please note that these questions and answers are only suggestions. Many other great questions could be asked to start helpful discussions, and other answers could be given for the questions that are asked below. So, be flexible, and enjoy the conversation.

1. In Book I, Marcus thanks a long list of people for a variety of things. Among them, he expresses gratitude for his education. What is he specifically thankful for? Why?

> In I.4, Marcus thanks his great-grandfather for not sending him to public schools, but being willing to provide great teachers at home (an ancient equivalent of homeschooling or private schooling). His great-grandfather taught him that a good education is worth the financial investment.

In I.17, Marcus thanks the gods for not letting academic achievement come too easily to him, lest he become overly engaged in them.

2. What is significant about Marcus writing much of his *Meditations* from a war camp?

This question has a variety of answers, but the reader should note that both Book I and Book II end with an inscription indicating that they were penned while on military campaigns. Perhaps Marcus' gratitude that his studies did not come too easily to him indicates that he maintained the ability to connect his education to real circumstances. He was no "ivory tower" thinker, separated from the consequences of his ideas. Rather, Marcus had to live out his philosophy in life or death situations, remaining faithful, dutiful, loyal, and calm in the face of battle.

3. Book II opens with the exhortation, "Begin the morning by saying to thyself, I shall meet with the busybody, the ungrateful, arrogant, deceitful, envious, unsocial. All these things happen to them by reason of their ignorance of what is good and evil." Do you agree that ignorance is the cause of people's wrong behavior? Why or why not?

This question should create some great discussion. Marcus says that the busybody, the ungrateful, arrogant, deceitful, and unsocial people we meet are the way they are because of their ignorance of good and evil. Ignorance simply means that they "do not know" good and evil. They do not understand how they are supposed to live.

For Christians, it is appropriate that we add that sin is about more than simple knowledge or lack of knowledge. Because of the fall of Adam, all men are born subject to sin (Psalm 51:5; Romans 3:23, 5:12; Ephesians 2:1-3). But, James 4:17 also says, "So whoever knows the right thing to do and fails to do it, for him it is sin." Knowledge and ignorance of the good, then, do play a role in how a person acts, and even in their guilt for acting or failing to act.

4. In II.8, Marcus writes that "those who do not observe the movements of their own minds must of necessity be unhappy." Why would he claim this? How would you respond?

    At his trial, Socrates said, "The unexamined life is not worth living." In Greek, Socrates said something more like, "The unexamined life is not fitting for a man." A true man must examine himself, his life, and "the movements of (his) mind." Scripture repeatedly commands men to do this. Consider Proverbs 3:21-26, 4:26, 5:6, 20:5.

5. Compare the *Meditations* with the book of Proverbs. How are they alike? How do they differ?

    This question is best discussed after students read a few selected chapters of Proverbs. It is helpful to include chapter 1 for reasons described below.

Both Meditations and Proverbs are works of wisdom literature (see "Understanding Wisdom Literature" for more on this), so they bear several similarities. Both address what it means to live skillfully—what to say, how to treat others, how to respond to difficult circumstances, how to control one's emotions, and so on.

However, the two works differ in significant ways as well. For example:

• Solomon addresses Proverbs to his "son," rather than recording his wisdom as an introspective work (a journal).

• Solomon sees God as the source of true wisdom, whereas Marcus only seems to pay the required homage to the gods.

• Solomon's Proverbs routinely remind the reader that life is lived with God in mind (which must affect this life as well), whereas Marcus' primary focus is on living wisely for the sake of a good life on this earth alone.

6. In III.4, Marcus begins, "Do not waste the remainder of thy life in thoughts about others, when thou dost not refer thy thoughts to some object of common utility." What kind of behavior is he discouraging? Why does he offer this advice to himself?

> Marcus is discouraging gossip, envy, being a busybody, and more. The remainder of III.4 gives his rationale: it is of no use to you or the other person, and it is a waste of time and energy that could be

used for better things. He also notes that, when we stop worrying about what everyone else is doing, we become less concerned with the criticisms of others.

7. Reread III.6. What does Marcus say about "praise from the many...power...enjoyment of pleasure"?

He warns himself never to choose those things above "that which is rationally and politically or practically good." By political good, he means good for the community, rather than politics in the modern sense. Perhaps most importantly, he cautions that choosing praise, power, or pleasure becomes increasingly easy each time we do it. So, "simply and freely choose the better, and hold to it."

8. Reread III.7. What does Marcus say about self-respect? Do you see that topic come up in other passages? If so, what does he say about it?

"Never value anything as profitable to thyself which shall compel thee to break thy promise, to lose thy self-respect, to hate any man, to suspect, to curse, to act the hypocrite, to desire anything which needs walls and curtains" (that is, needs to be hidden because of the shame it would bring upon you). Throughout *Meditations*, Marcus stresses the need to be a good man so you can live with self-respect, regardless of what others think of you or what hardships you face. Students may bring up many different lines or passages, all of which could be explored with the topic of self-respect in mind.

9. As we saw in the previous question, Marcus wrote,
    "Never value anything as profitable to thyself which
    shall compel thee to break thy promise, to lose thy
    self-respect, to hate any man, to suspect, to curse, to act
    the hypocrite, to desire anything which needs walls and
    curtains" (III.7). Compare his list with the "fruit of the
    Spirit" in Galatians 5:22-23. How are they alike? How
    do they differ?

    > Marcus' list overlaps a good deal with the "fruit
    > of the Spirit" (love, peace, kindness, faithfulness,
    > gentleness, self-control), but Marcus would likely
    > define them differently. Additionally, he seems
    > motivated more by personal benefit than love for
    > his neighbor, but it should be noted that personal
    > benefit is not entirely wrong in this case.

10. What is the difference between self-respect and pride?
    Use Marcus' words to inform your answer.

    > Self-respect means living above reproach, in a way
    > that is honorable. By doing so, we can know that
    > any disrespect or dishonor we receive is undeserved.
    > A person with self-respect can hear criticism and
    > see how they might improve, while pride causes
    > one to assume he "has it all together" and doesn't
    > need any improvement. In other words, self-respect
    > drives a person to become better, while pride causes
    > one to think he doesn't need to be better. Pride
    > also causes a person to look down on others, while
    > self-respect would require treating others honorably.

11. What is the difference between self-respect, as described by Marcus, and "self-esteem" as we typically think of it?

> The modern concept of "self-esteem" generally focuses on how we feel about ourselves, sometimes without asking how we *should* feel about ourselves. Often, talk of self-esteem encourages us to feel good about ourselves no matter what, regardless of whether our lives are honorable and good or not. Self-esteem, then, is often motivated by pride.

12. In IV.3, Marcus wrote that "men do wrong involuntarily." How would you respond to this? Do you agree or disagree? Why?

> This question is similar to number 3, addressing the claim that people do evil out of "ignorance." Here he says they do it "involuntarily." Answers to this question will necessarily vary, but there are some thoughts worth considering. If people really understood their actions as "wrong," would they still do it? That's not to say some people aren't attracted to bad things, but if they really understood that they are *wrong*, would they do them? Could we argue that this is precisely why some people work so hard to call evil, good and good, evil? They need their actions to be seen as acceptable because, perhaps deep down, they do not want to do what is genuinely wrong. Another interesting thought experiment is to compare Marcus' assertion with Paul's words in Romans 7:13-25.

13. Compare the first sentence in IV.49 with Jesus' words in Matthew 7:24-27.

> The passages are similar in the images used—being established on a rock, facing the storms of life and being unmoved, etc. Both acknowledge that life will bring storms and withstanding them is difficult. However, it may prove helpful to contrast that Jesus says this is only possible with a life established on Him and His teachings, while Marcus makes no references to God or the gods as being necessary. What would Marcus' rock be? Himself alone?

14. In V.16, Marcus says that some thoughts must become "habitual." As an example, he says, "where a man can live, there he can also live well. But he must live in a palace; well then, he can also live well in a palace." Why would Marcus find it difficult to live in a palace? What do you think he means by living well?

> Marcus repeatedly warns about the dangers of living for wealth, power, and pleasure, so life in a palace would be a life full of temptation. So, he finds it necessary to "dye" these encouragements to live well in his soul, to make them "habitual thoughts." By living well, Marcus means living a life of self-control and discipline, pursuing the ideal of being a "good" man, regardless of his circumstances or temptations.

15. Compare VI.2 with Philippians 4:11-13. VI.2 says, "Let it make no difference to thee whether thou art cold or

warm, if thou art doing thy duty; and whether thou art drowsy or satisfied with sleep; and whether ill-spoken of or praised; and whether dying or doing something else. For it is one of the acts of life, this act by which we die: it is sufficient then in this act also to do well what we have in hand."

> Both passages address the need to learn and practice contentment, regardless of whether one's circumstances are good or bad. Both encourage us to accept what comes to us as an opportunity to do the right thing. As with question 13, it may also be helpful to ask where the strength for contentment comes from—for both Marcus and for Paul.

16. "It is in our power to have no opinion about a thing, and not to be disturbed in our soul; for things themselves have no natural power to form our judgments" (VI.52). How do we learn to follow this advice in our age, when opinions are made accessible through so many means?

> Social media (Facebook, Twitter, etc.), 24-hour news, comment sections, and a 24-hour worldwide news cycle make expressing our every thought and opinion quick and simple. But at what cost? Many of our opinions are not well-considered or thought out, and will change with time. Additionally, sometimes the desire to express all of our opinions is really just a lack of self-control, and we need to learn to hold our tongues (or our typing fingers).

Sometimes it is better to simply let a matter go and say nothing. Why disturb our souls over every issue?

17. In VIII.9, Marcus wrote, "Let no man any longer hear thee finding fault with the court life or with thy own." People can find fault in their circumstances, even when living "court life." Why do we find it so easy to complain? What is to be done about it?

> For Christians, the answer is repentance for our ingratitude and thanklessness. But, as Marcus taught himself, we also would benefit from making gratitude a "habitual thought," training ourselves to be thankful and refrain from complaining.

18. Name at least one passage from the *Meditations* that stands out to you. Why is it important to you? What did you learn from it?

> Answers will vary.

19. Marcus Aurelius, while being a wise man, persecuted Christians as the Roman emperor. What impact does that have on you as a Christian reading his *Meditations*?

> Answers will vary here, but it is important to wrestle with this question. Marcus was wise, but, like Solomon, he certainly was not perfect. His wisdom was a gift of common grace (that is, a gift of God's goodness, even to an unbeliever), so it is real and profitable for us, but Marcus was also a pagan, so his wisdom must be held up against the wisdom of

God and His Word. This question also leads to the broader discussion of why Christians should read the classics, even when written by pagans. They are of great benefit because God gives gifts to all men, even unbelievers, and Christians are able to profit from those gifts, even when they are flawed in other senses.

20. Church historian Philip Schaff wrote, "The *Meditations* of Marcus Aurelius are full of beautiful moral maxims, strung together without system. They bear a striking resemblance to Christian ethics."[19] Do you agree? Why or why not?

Obviously, this question does not have a "right" answer, but responses should be rooted in what Marcus wrote. His writings do bear close parallels with Christian ethics in places, and they differ from Christian ethics in places, so both should be pointed out.

21. What are the most important lessons you will take from reading the *Meditations*?

Answers will vary.

---

19   *History of the Christian Church*, 2:328.

FURTHER DISCUSSION AND REVIEW

Master what you have read by reviewing and integrating the different elements of this classic.

AUTHOR AND SETTING
Be able to describe the life and career of Marcus Aurelius. Also, be able to summarize how that relates to his principles, and explain whether that makes you respect him more or not.

ARGUMENT
Be able to describe the major teachings of the book along with specific details about what makes them compelling or interesting. This includes both things that you agree and disagree with.

PHILOSOPHICAL ISSUES

Be able to describe what this classic is telling us about the world. Is the message true? What truth can we take from the argument and philosophical questions discussed? What kind of influence has Aurelius had on history? Finally, be able to interact with the following philosophical and practical questions (or any others you've noticed) from this classic:

- How does man relate to the gods?
- Do men have free will or are their lives "fated"?
- How do we find the proper balance between duty and personal responsibility?
- How should we react to difficult people and circumstances?
- What does it mean to be a man?
- When should we feel sorrow or happiness?
- How can we be content and grateful?

Finally, identify another philosophical issue, large or small, in this classic. Use the Bible and common sense to evaluate the Stoic approach to that issue. If you need it, you can use the list of key issues on pages 13–14 as a starting point.

A NOTE FROM THE PUBLISHER:
TAKING THE CLASSICS QUIZ

Once you have finished the worldview guide, you can prepare for the end-of-book test. Each test will consist of a short-answer section on the book itself and the author, a short-answer section on plot and the narrative, and a long-answer essay section on worldview, conflict, and themes.

Each quiz, along with other helps, can be downloaded for free at www.canonpress.com/ClassicsQuizzes. If you have any questions about the quiz or its answers or the Worldview Guides in general, you can contact Canon Press at service@canonpress.com or 208.892.8074.

www.ingramcontent.com/pod-product-compliance
Lightning Source LLC
Chambersburg PA
CBHW071936020426
42331CB00010B/2891